What is a
top predator?

Bobbie Kalman

Crabtree Publishing Company

www.crabtreebooks.com

Big
Science Ideas

Created by Bobbie Kalman

For my cousin Heather Brissenden
You are beautiful, intelligent, and such a great spirit!
Peter and I love you very much.

Author and
Editor-in-Chief
Bobbie Kalman

Editor
Kathy Middleton

Proofreader
Crystal Sikkens

Photo research
Bobbie Kalman

Design
Bobbie Kalman
Katherine Berti
Samantha Crabtree
    (logo and front cover)

Print and production coordinator
Katherine Berti

Prepress technician
Katherine Berti

Illustrations
Bonna Rouse: page 20 (lemmings)

Photographs
BigStockPhoto: page 19 (top left)
Comstock: page 30 (milk)
Eyewire: page 11 (bottom)
Photodisc: page 31 (bottom fruits and vegetables)
Wikimedia Commons: Linda Tanner: page 11 (top left)
All other images by Shutterstock

Library and Archives Canada Cataloguing in Publication

Kalman, Bobbie
    What is a top predator? / Bobbie Kalman.

(Big science ideas)
Includes index.
Issued also in electronic formats.
ISBN 978-0-7787-2772-9 (bound).--ISBN 978-0-7787-2777-4 (pbk.)

    1. Top predators--Juvenile literature. 2. Predatory animals--
Juvenile literature. I. Title. II. Series: Kalman, Bobbie. Big
science ideas.

QL758.K34 2012   j591.5'3   C2011-907685-3

Library of Congress Cataloging-in-Publication Data

Kalman, Bobbie.
    What is a top predator? / Bobbie Kalman.
        p. cm. -- (Big science ideas)
    Includes index.
    ISBN 978-0-7787-2772-9 (reinforced library binding : alk. paper) -- ISBN 978-
0-7787-2777-4 (pbk. : alk. paper) -- ISBN 978-1-4271-7841-1 (electronic pdf) --
ISBN 978-1-4271-7956-2 (electronic html)
    1. Top predators--Juvenile literature. 2. Predatory animals--Juvenile
literature. I. Title.

QL758.K35 2012
591.5'3--dc23

2011046111

Crabtree Publishing Company

www.crabtreebooks.com   1-800-387-7650

Printed in Canada/012012/MA20111130

Published in Canada
Crabtree Publishing
616 Welland Ave.
St. Catharines, Ontario
L2M 5V6

Published in the United States
Crabtree Publishing
PMB 59051
350 Fifth Avenue, 59th Floor
New York, New York 10118

Published in the United Kingdom
Crabtree Publishing
Maritime House
Basin Road North, Hove
BN41 1WR

Published in Australia
Crabtree Publishing
3 Charles Street
Coburg North
VIC 3058

Contents

What is a top predator?

A **predator** is an animal that hunts and eats other animals. The animals predators hunt are called **prey**. A **top predator** is a predator that is not prey to other predators in its **habitat**, or natural home. For example, polar bears eat other animals, but no animals hunt and eat polar bears. Top predators are also known as **apex predators**. "Apex" means the highest point of something. Apex predators are at the highest point of the **food chain** in their habitats. A food chain is the pattern of one living thing eating another living thing (see next page).

Some animals, like this coyote, are apex predators in some habitats, but not in others.

wolf

Coyotes are apex predators in many habitats but not in habitats where wolves hunt.

What is a food chain?

All living things need **energy**. Energy is the power living things need to stay alive. Energy starts with the sun. The sun's energy is passed along to living things through food. Plants use sunlight, water, and air to make food. Making food from sunlight is called **photosynthesis**. Animals cannot make their own food. They get their energy from eating other living things such as plants or other animals.

Energy in food

The food chain on the right shows a plant, a rabbit, and a cougar. The cougar is the last link in this food chain. It is a top predator in several habitats.

sun's energy

Plants use the sun's energy to make food.

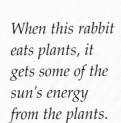

When this rabbit eats plants, it gets some of the sun's energy from the plants.

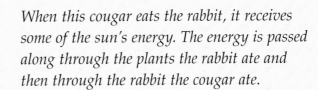

When this cougar eats the rabbit, it receives some of the sun's energy. The energy is passed along through the plants the rabbit ate and then through the rabbit the cougar ate.

5

The energy pyramid

When animals eat, energy is passed along from the sun, to plants, and then through animals. This energy **pyramid** shows the flow of energy. A pyramid is a triangle that is wide at the bottom and has sides that meet at the top in a point. At the bottom are many plants. On the next level are **herbivores**, or animals that eat mainly plants. The animals that eat herbivores are **carnivores**. Most carnivores are predators. Some are **omnivores** that eat both plants and other animals.

Note: Read the information on page 6 from bottom to top.

Carnivores

The top level of the energy pyramid is the narrowest. There are even fewer carnivores than there are plants or other kinds of animals. Some carnivores are top predators, and some are eaten by top predators. Eagles, wolves, lynxes, cougars, and polar bears are top predators.

Herbivores

Herbivores must eat many plants to get the energy they need. There are fewer herbivores than plants, so the energy pyramid is narrower at this level of the food chain. Herbivores are not top predators because they do not hunt animals.

Plants

The first level of a food chain is made up of plants. There are many more plants than there are animals because it takes many plants to feed all the animals in a food chain.

Flow of e

eagle

cougar

polar bear

wolf

lynx

Flow of energy

butterfly

goose

mouse

lamb

deer

cardinal

prairie
dog

squirrel

rabbit

7

Producers and consumers

Plants are at the bottom of the energy pyramid. They are called **primary producers** because they are the **primary**, or first, links in a food chain, and they **produce**, or make, food. Herbivores are the next level up in the energy pyramid and are called **primary consumers**. They are the first living things in the food chain to **consume**, or eat, food to get energy. At the top of the energy pyramid are carnivores that eat herbivores. They are called **secondary consumers** because they eat primary consumers. Carnivores that eat other carnivores, or secondary consumers, are called **tertiary**, or third, consumers.

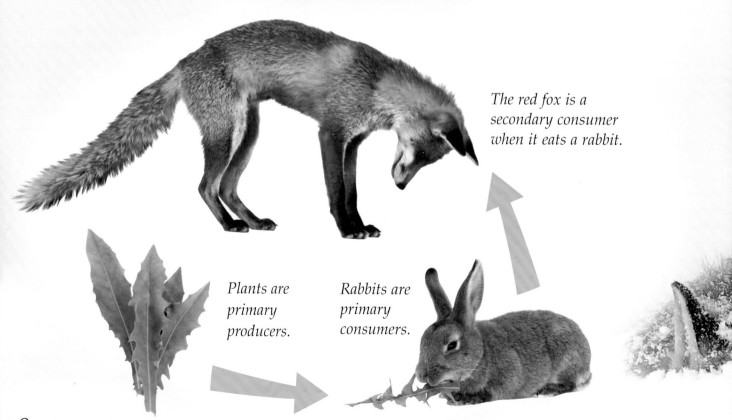

The red fox is a secondary consumer when it eats a rabbit.

Plants are primary producers.

Rabbits are primary consumers.

This eagle has found a dead fox to eat. It is a tertiary consumer when it eats the fox, which has eaten a rabbit. It is also a top predator because it is not hunted by other predators.

Prairie top predators

rabbit

prairie dog

Grasslands are mostly flat lands where grasses and other small plants grow. Some grasslands have a few trees. **Prairies** are grasslands that are found in Canada and the United States. Prairies can have short or long grasses and flowers, but very few trees. Prairie grasses feed many herbivores, such as mice, rabbits, mule deer, prairie dogs, and ground squirrels. These animals are then eaten by bobcats, foxes, coyotes, and hawks.

This baby bobcat will be a top predator when it becomes an adult. As a baby, it may be eaten by other predators.

Wolves in prairies eat large animals such as bison and elk. They also kill and may eat coyotes and red foxes when these carnivores are hunting the same prey.

Coyotes are top predators in the prairies, except in areas where there are wolves.

Red-tailed hawks are top prairie predators. They are also secondary and tertiary consumers that eat herbivores and other carnivores.

Adult bobcats are top prairie predators. This bobcat is a secondary consumer because it eats jackrabbits.

A cougar is a top predator. This cougar is hunting a badger, which is a carnivore. The cougar is a tertiary consumer because it eats badgers.

Savanna top predators

Savannas are large grasslands in areas where the weather is hot all year. Many animals feed on the grasses, shrubs, and trees that grow in savannas. Some very big herbivores live on the savannas in Africa. They are elephants, giraffes, rhinoceroses, and hippopotamuses. Other herbivores are antelopes and zebras. The top predators that live on the savanna hunt most of these animals. Lions are top predators that often hunt in groups to kill big animals such as zebras, wildebeest, and sometimes even elephant calves.

giraffe

antelope

zebra

This mother lion is taking her cubs on a hunt. She will teach them how to chase and take down prey. Prey are the animals that predators hunt.

Big wild cats

Lions, cheetahs, and leopards are big cats. They are all top predators. Cheetahs are fast runners that can outrun most prey. Leopards can run fast, too, and they can climb trees while carrying heavy prey such as antelopes.

antelope

leopard

cheetah

wolf

Forest top predators

Forests are habitats in which many plants grow. The largest plants are the tall trees that make up most forests. Other forest plants include bushes, flowers, and grasses. There are plenty of leaves, grasses, seeds, and nuts for herbivores to eat in a forest. Forest herbivores include squirrels, deer, chipmunks, beavers, porcupines, and many kinds of birds and insects. Carnivores such as frogs and toads, foxes, owls, and weasels, also live in forests. They eat the herbivores.

fox

owl

Chipmunks and squirrels are forest herbivores. Owls and foxes eat chipmunks and squirrels.

eagle

Top predators

The top predators in forests include eagles, wolves, lynxes, and brown bears. Not all these predators live in the same forests.

Lynxes live in forest habitats. They eat mice, rabbits, and birds. Sometimes they hunt deer, too. This lynx is eating a bird.

(below) Brown bears are omnivores. They eat plants, as well as other animals. Brown bears especially like fish. They are top predators because no other animals hunt them.

Wolves are top predators. They hunt large animals such as deer and moose. They sometimes kill and eat coyotes if they are competing for the same food.

Rainforest top predators

Top predators in **rain forests** include jaguars, leopards, tigers, and big snakes. A rain forest is a forest that gets a lot of rain. **Tropical rain forests** are in areas where the weather is hot all year. Some tropical rain forests, such as the Amazon rain forest in South America, get rain every day. The Amazon rain forest has the most **species**, or types, of plants and animals on Earth. There are also huge rain forests in Africa and Asia, which have **rainy seasons**, when it rains every day, and **dry seasons**, when it does not rain for months.

Boa constrictors are long snakes that can eat huge prey, including other predators such as ocelots.

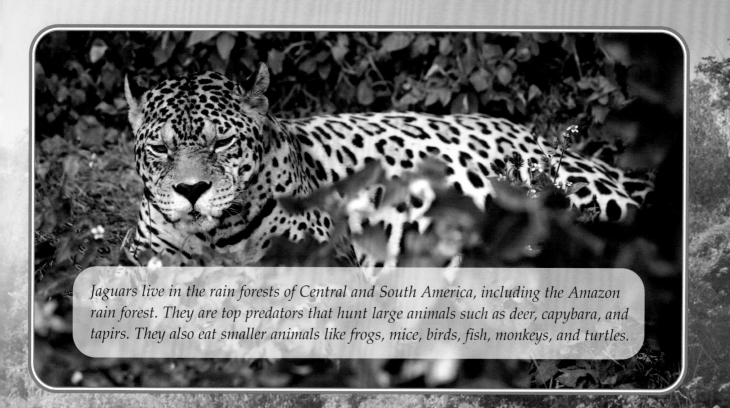

Jaguars live in the rain forests of Central and South America, including the Amazon rain forest. They are top predators that hunt large animals such as deer, capybara, and tapirs. They also eat smaller animals like frogs, mice, birds, fish, monkeys, and turtles.

Sumatran tigers live in the tropical forests of Sumatra, Indonesia, a country in Asia. They are top predators that hunt wild boar, deer, and smaller animals, like birds, monkeys, and fish. They are very **endangered** animals (see pages 28–29).

Mountain top predators

Mountains are areas of rocky land with steep sides that rise almost straight up from the ground. Foxes, coyotes, cougars, and wolves are some predators that live on mountains. Birds such as eagles and hawks fly above mountains, looking for prey to eat. Mountain goats, bighorn sheep, and rabbits are prey to these predators.

bighorn lamb

Mountain lions, also known as cougars, are top predators. They hunt bighorn sheep and their lambs, rabbits, and many other animals.

Coyotes are top predators, unless there are wolves in the same area.

Red foxes are predators that are sometimes eaten by top predators.

Wolves are top predators. They hunt large prey in **packs**, or groups.

19

Arctic top predators

The Arctic is at the top of Earth. It is a cold place with snow and ice. Lemmings, arctic hares, caribou, and ground squirrels are herbivores that are eaten by predators on the arctic **tundra**. The tundra is a huge area of frozen land, where winter lasts for most of the year. Arctic top predators include brown bears, polar bears, snowy owls, arctic foxes, and arctic wolves. Some arctic predators live on the tundra, and some, such as the orca, live in the Arctic Ocean (see page 22).

*Snowy owls are top predators, but their **owlets**, or baby owls, are sometimes eaten by arctic foxes and wolves.*

Arctic hares can dig through snow in winter to find plants to eat. Hares are eaten by many predators.

lemming

caribou

Arctic wolves eat caribou, rabbits, birds, lemmings, and other land animals.

Brown bears are omnivores. They are also top predators because no other arctic animal hunts them.

Polar bears are top predators that hunt and eat fish, seals, and whales in the Arctic Ocean. This polar bear is hunting a seal.

Top predators in oceans

Oceans are huge areas of **salt water**. Salt water contains a lot of salt. Some oceans are in parts of the world with hot weather. Some oceans, such as the Arctic Ocean, are in parts of the world with cold weather. Fish and other kinds of animals live in oceans. Many ocean animals are carnivores. Carnivores that live in the **coral reefs** of warm oceans eat fish and **corals**. In other parts of oceans, carnivores eat seals, whales, dolphins, and sea turtles.

*This giant moray eel is a kind of fish.
It is a top predator in coral reefs, like
this one. It eats mainly lobsters,
shrimps, and crabs.*

corals

orca

bottlenose
dolphin

tiger shark

great white
shark

Top ocean predators include many kinds of
sharks, such as great white sharks and tiger
sharks. Most sharks are tertiary consumers.
They eat other carnivores such as seals and
dolphins. Orcas are top predators in many
oceans. They are large dolphins that eat seals,
sharks, sea lions, sea otters, and other dolphins.

seal

Predators in fresh water

Some animals live in **fresh water**. Fresh water does not contain very much salt. Lakes, rivers, ponds, and some **wetlands** contain fresh water. Wetlands are lands that are covered in water for all or part of the year. Many kinds of fish, frogs, and turtles live in freshwater habitats. Alligators, crocodiles, and river dolphins are top predators that also live in freshwater habitats. They eat small and large prey that they find in the water and on land near water.

The Nile crocodile lives in the Nile River in Africa, as well as in African lakes and wetlands. It is a top predator. This crocodile has caught a fish to eat, but crocodiles also hunt large prey on land, such as young hippos, zebras, and antelopes.

The Amazon river dolphin is the largest river dolphin. It has about 100 front teeth for catching prey. It eats crabs, shrimp, small turtles, and many kinds of fish. This dolphin is a top predator in the Amazon River.

American alligators are top predators that live in wetlands in the southern United States. They can run quickly on land to catch large prey.

Very important animals!

Predators are very important members of food chains. When there are no predators in a habitat, too many herbivores are born. Too many herbivores eat all the plants in an area. Many animals starve. Predators, especially top predators, keep the **population**, or numbers, of herbivores in balance. There is then enough food for both herbivores and carnivores.

deer tick

Too many deer in an area can strip the bark off trees, eat most of the wild plants, and raid people's gardens for food. Deer can also carry dangerous ticks, which cause diseases.

Healthy herds

Predators also keep animal **herds**, or large groups, healthy because they often hunt sick or old animals. When the old and sick members are gone, there is more food for the younger, healthier members of the herd.

This mother lion has hunted an old zebra. The zebra will feed the lion and all her cubs. One of the cubs is eating the zebra with her.

Endangered top predators

When you look at the energy pyramid on pages 6–7, you can see that there are fewer top predators than there are herbivores. For this reason, many top predators are endangered. Some are **critically endangered** and will become **extinct** unless people protect them. Sharks, polar bears, and many kinds of whales are endangered ocean hunters. Top predators on land, such as tigers, panthers, lions, and leopards, are endangered because they are losing their habitats. Many of these predators are also being hunted by people.

This Sumatran tiger cub is critically endangered and may soon become extinct.

Lions are losing their habitats. They are also being hunted for sport.

Polar bears are endangered because Earth is getting warmer, and the ice in oceans is melting. Polar bears need to drag their prey out of the ocean and onto ice to eat it.

Losing leopards

Leopards are beautiful wild cats with spotted fur. There are eight species of leopards, and all are endangered. Farmers often kill leopards to protect their farm animals from being eaten by these cats. Leopards are also hunted for their fur, bones, whiskers, and meat. Many leopards live in **preserves**, or special parks that protect animals.

This snow leopard is endangered because it is losing its habitat. It is also being hunted by farmers.

The Amur leopard is one of the most endangered animals in the world. There are only 30–40 of these cats alive in the wild. The forests where they live are being burned by farmers, and some Amur leopards are shot by hunters. These cats may soon become extinct.

Human top predators

Humans are top predators because they eat animals and are not hunted by other predators. Some people hunt or catch the animals they eat, and others raise animals on farms. Not all people eat meat, but most are omnivores that eat both plant and animal foods. They eat the eggs, milk products, and meat of animals. Humans eat some animals and endanger others by taking over the **wilderness** areas where animals live. When animals lose their homes, they lose their food, too, and many die. Humans also **pollute**, or dirty, the water and land on which some animals live. Many animals die from pollution caused by people.

This man has caught a huge fish. Fish are a source of food for people. People are catching too many fish, however, leaving top predators in oceans and lakes without food.

Are you more of a carnivore or herbivore? Studies show that eating more vegetables and fruit is better for your health than eating too much meat. Fruits and vegetables grown near where you live are the best because they are fresher. You could even grow a vegetable garden at your home. A few plants will feed your family all summer long!

Glossary

Note: Some boldfaced words are defined where they appear in the book.

carnivore An animal that eats other animals

coral Small animals that live in oceans and stay only in one place

coral reef A large underwater structure that is made up of tiny animals called coral polyps

critically endangered Describes animals that are at high risk of dying out

endangered Describes animals that are in danger of dying out

extinct Describes animals that no longer live anywhere on Earth

food chain A pattern of eating and being eaten

habitat The natural place where an animal lives

herbivore An animal that eats mainly plant foods

omnivore An animal that eats plants and animals

predator An animal that hunts and eats other animals

preserve A natural area set aside by a country's government to protect the plants and wild animals living in that area

prey An animal that is eaten by another animal

primary consumer The first living thing that eats food to get energy

primary producer A green plant, which is the first food maker in a food chain

secondary consumer A living thing that eats primary consumers to get energy

tertiary consumer Tertiary means third; tertiary consumers are the third group of living things that eat to get energy from food

wilderness Natural places where plants and animals live, which are not controlled by people

Index